Introduction

As a Network Marketer you already know the power of the compounding effect and passive income. You understand the power of building a solid customer base which buys from you on a regular basis. You understand the power of duplication and teach that to others by building successful teams which in turn generates passive income. You already know it take lots patience, determination and focus to achieve these results. You also understand you can't be an instant success but that it takes lots of little steps over and over again and your rewards is building a successful business which generates a great deal of passive income. However, did you know you use exactly the same skills to building an investment portfolio which will produce passive income year after year?

Network Marketing is a cash rich business model, but once you are making money from your business do you know what to invest your surplus money into or how to invest the cash to generate even greater wealth? Think of investing as another leg in your Network Marketing business. It's a leg in which your team will consist of pounds and pennies or dollars and cents and they will be working hard to generate wealth and lifestyle for you.

My name is Karen Newton and I'm an Investor. I borrowed £300 on a credit card and turned it into £10 million in 4 years using the systems covered in this book. I've developed investment strategies and systems that anyone can follow. I call it "From Zero to Millionaire". This system is designed to help potential investors start with absolutely no money and go 'From Zero to Millionaire'. As a Network Marketer you already have a head start over of other people who invest in this system. You have a proven business model to generate wealth.

Nothing in this book is theory this is the actual system that I used to build both lifestyle and wealth. It is the same system I teach my clients and their successes have been phenomenal. One member became financially free within 8 months. Other members have created financial independence in 12-18 months. What can you do?

I have been an author of investment books for 16 years. In 2015, I was approached by a buyer of one of my books to provide private investment coaching. That person, Peter Rowlands, then suggested I could help some people he knew and the £2.73 Club was formed. Since working with Peter he has become a very successful investor and my business partner.

Through the £2.73 Club we now offer an array of off training programs in Shares; Property; Business and Cash investing or our Mastermind monthly training program. Our investment systems are used by hundreds of people who are making changes to their finances and lifestyle.

Here's what just a few have to say.

Connecting with Karen has changed my life. Karen has an accessible style, you can relate to her easily, she can captivate an audience and provides the steps which build a bridge for individuals to use in order to move from where they are now to where they want to be. Participating in the £2.73 Club has caused a paradigm shift in my own thinking about business and now a whole new future lays before me. Karen changes the lives of those ready to take action, she makes wealth accessible to everyone. - **Marilyn Maidment – Director EquipYou Ltd**

Karen's wealth of knowledge and experience gives an audience something to pay attention to and learn from. Karen is a generous, supportive and helpful lady whose willingness to help others through her £2.73 Club makes her someone you really should get to know. - **Penny Jarman – Business Development Office at QualitySolicitors Rubin Lewis O'Brien**

Karen's wealth of knowledge and understanding of many businesses is interesting and inspiring. Overcoming adversity and representing women in non-traditional sectors resonates with our members. Thank you Karen for sharing your journey and showing a 'can do' attitude is everything! **Bethan Baldwin, Pride of Britain Fundraiser of the year 2015**

I joined Karen's £2.73 mastermind last year and have learned so much about investing in her 4 categories. She says she can take you from zero to a million and she isn't kidding. Her mastermind group is a structured and proven formula that you can follow while also having the autonomy to explore new investments and ask her advice on these. I'm enjoying the learning and financial growth that being part of Karen's mastermind group provides. **Natasha Davies, Global Mindset Coach, Consultant and Author**

Fantastic book started reading it and couldn't put it down. Read the whole book in two days and ended up with bits of paper sticking out of the book at various points with pages I wanted to go back to. It's inspired me to make changes in my life. If you are looking to make a change in your financial future I highly recommend this book. **Peter Rowlands, P&M360 Photography, Storyteller. - Peter was talking about the book 'Surviving 2013' since reading the book he became a private coached client and is now a director of The £2.73 Club Limited**

Been investing for years with no balance and over exposed in certain areas, now starting to finally get it, little steps and a lot of help and advice from Karen Newton I can begin to see the light at the end of the tunnel... **Michael Wheatle, Property Investor**

Just back from the Zero to Millionaire Seminar, What an amazing day, lots of great advice, tips and expertise, fantastic speakers and faultless knowledge, I am looking forward to putting into practice some of what I have learnt today. Thanks Again - **Steve Gregory, S Care Training Ltd**

Schools in the UK teach a little about budgeting and compound interest but not the skill of using it in real life to generate wealth. Why should they, when most schools only teach you how to work for someone else? Once you grow up and start work the only learning you do is if you make a conscience effort to attend a seminar. Mainly those seminars are aimed at upselling products and services. At the £2.73 Club we take a different approach. We've gone back to the school environment by teach investing in monthly classes with homework in between. A step by step process that once learnt will stay with you for life. A back to basics approach. The basics being:-

- Learning Investing skills. Skills help you make the right decision and see opportunities around you.
- Learning what constitutes an investment - understanding what an investment is ensures you buy the right type of investments.
- Learning the mind-set. It's a way of looking at things differently and assessing the opportunities.
- Learning the language. Understand the language and you understand the world of money.

As a Network Marketer you are already working and investing in one category – Business. You have a major head start over some of my clients who start with nothing.

In this book you will learn about other investment strategies that can be implemented to make sure your hard worked for income goes much further. You'll also learn how Network Marketing fits into this strategy.

Investing is simply about having your money work for you instead of you having to work for money.

Network Marketing is the first step on the road to creating incredible wealth and lifestyle. Now we'll show you the subsequent steps of investing and how to have your money work for you.

For more information about the £2.73 Club and how we can help you with your investment skills visit our Facebook page

www.facebook.com/273ClubLimited

Legal

The right of Karen Newton to be identified as Author has been asserted in accordance with the Copyright, Designs and Patent Act 1988

© 2018 Karen Newton.

All rights reserved. No part of this book may be reproduced, stored in a retrieval system, or in any form or by any means, without the prior permission in writing of the author.

Disclaimer: To the fullest extent permitted by law. Karen Newton is providing this written material, its subsidiary elements and its contents on an 'as is' basis and makes no (and expressly disclaim all) representations or warranties of any kind with respect to this written material or its contents including, without limitation, advice and recommendations, warranties or merchantability and fitness for a particular purpose. The information is given for entertainment purpose only – in addition Karen Newton does not represent or warrant that the information accessible via this written material is accurate, complete or current. To the fullest extent permitted by law, Karen Newton or any of her affiliates, partners, employees or other representatives will not be liable for damages arising out of or in connection with the use of this written material. This is a comprehensive limitation of liability that applies to all damages of any kind including (without limitation) compensatory, direct, indirect or consequential damages, loss of date, income or profit, loss of or damage to property and claims of third parties.

The Basics

Pyramid Investing

Yikes, she wants me to start a pyramid scheme. I wonder how often you've heard that while building your Network Marketing business. Well, I get that all the time when I talk about Pyramid Investing and no it's not a pyramid scheme. It is simply a way to demonstrate how building in all four investment categories and layering the skills and knowledge will help you generate enormous wealth.

Over 5000 years ago the Egyptians built pyramids. Solid, stable four sided structures that have stood the test of time and survived for thousands of years. They have endured all the weather conditions that have battered them over the years. As I write this book, yet another pyramid has been unearthed in Egypt. This pyramid is said to be even older than the Great Pyramid at Giza and thought to be even bigger.

So, you are going to build a pyramid of investments that no matter what the economic climate, they will have potential for growth and continue providing you with a steady income in the ups and downs of the market.

4 Category Investing

Above is the aerial view of our Investment Pyramid. It has 4 sides or 4 categories in which to start building investments – Cash, Paper, Business and Property. Each side of the Investment Pyramid has numerous options in which you can invest. As you build up your skills and knowledge the number of investments and types of investment available open up to you. Let's look at the 4 investment categories. Don't worry if you don't understand them they are covered in more detail in the book.

Cash – this includes Bullion, Peer-to-Peer lending, Treasury Bonds, and Fixed Term Deposits. These are usually, low performing stable investments. They counter the volatility of other investments and turbulent economic times.

Paper – is an investment where you hand your money over and receive a receipt in exchange. These types of investments are Shares, Gilts (Government and Corporate Bonds), ETF (Electronic Traded Funds) ETC (Electronic Traded Commodities) and Managed Funds. In the £2.73 Club we start with an investment strategy that is low risk and low management time while you learn the skills of investing in paper assets.

Business – an investment business is anything you have set up but no longer need to work in. Think of Richard Branson and Virgin as an example of investment businesses. He has around 400 businesses which it is impossible to work in but which still generate healthy returns for him. With an investment business it takes work every day to get the business started. Once you have built it to a certain level it can be run without your day to day involvement. As a large number of people do not have skills to run an investment type business the best way forward for them is either Network Marketing or Franchising. Both these business models are about building large businesses, with huge turnover generating excess cash without all the work being placed on one person.

Property – covers all types of investments where you own something that someone else wants to rent. Residential, Commercial, Holiday Lets, Garages are just some examples. We will also be looking at strategies that allow you to own property with little or no money such as Lease Options, Rent-to-Rent, Rent-to-buy, Delayed Completion and Joint Ventures.

The Glue

Holding our Pyramid together is the glue (pillars). There are 4 different types of glues. Fundamental Analysis, Technical Analysis, Risk Management and Cashflow.

Fundamental Analysis – is analysing the current situation of an investment. How sound is this investment? Based on current information do you think this will be okay to invest in today? As an example of some questions to ask yourself - if buying shares is it a sound company you are investing in. Will it provide a regular dividend or the growth you want? With property you are asking yourself is this something someone will want to rent. Do rental ratios work? What that means is if you are borrowing money to buy the property will you get the expected rent to cover the repayments? So, fundamental analysis is looking at the now.

Technical Analysis - is looking at the future. With shares this is looking at competition and the future of the product. Will the company continue growing has it reached its peak? Reading and understanding Charts and being able to see trends. Property is looking at the town or city. Growth potential and demand for the type of property you are investing in. Schools opening and closing. Employment in the region. Again looking at charts to see where price movements are going. These are all examples of Technical Analysis.

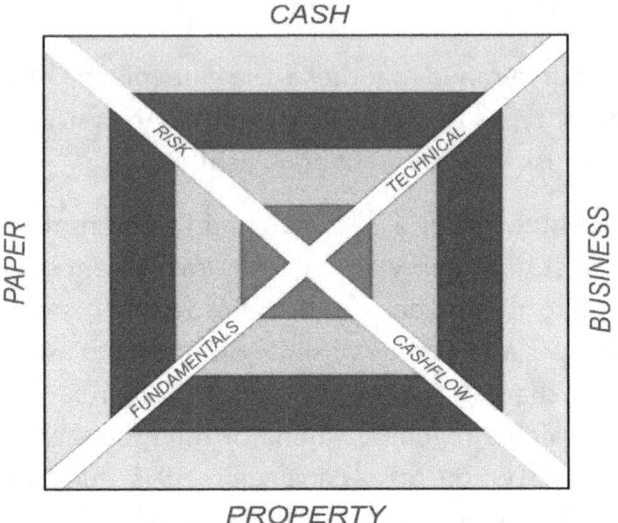

Risk Management – is as it says, managing the risk of the investment. For property this could include having property insurance, loss of rent insurance. Insurance to cover damage to the property. Do you want to manage yourself or have someone else manage it for you? With shares we reduce the risk of loss by using Stop Loss tools and protecting the amount of cash we have at risk. We also use Bullion as a Hedge. Hedge means investing in something else in case another investment falters. In poor economic times gold and silver will usually go up while other investments go down. We are protecting ourselves and our assets.

Cashflow – ensuring you have enough cash to be able to support your investment. Being able to guarantee sufficient income from the investment. Generating more cash to be able to put money into more investments. You also want enough cash coming in to ensure you can have the type of lifestyle you want and be able to afford it.

Stacking (or Layering) Investments

Stacking Investments means you are building multiple investments in each side of the Pyramid. Each investment is there for a different purpose. To understand Stacking let's look at the side view of the Investment Pyramid.

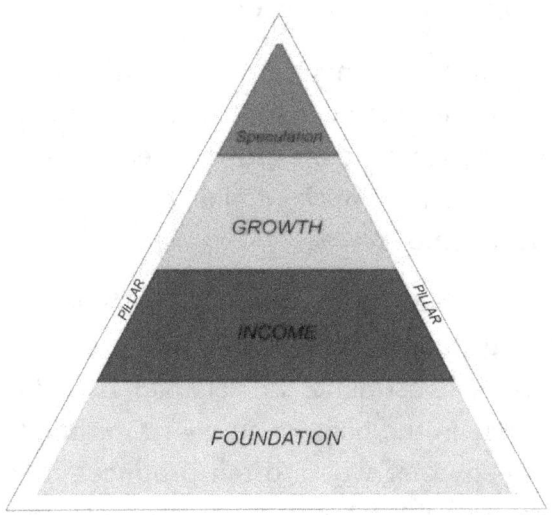

Again there are 4 parts (Stack/Layers) in the pyramid. The stacks are Foundation, Income, Growth and Speculation. The way to remember this is FIGS.

Foundation – The foundation is where you start to build the foundation on which you will be building your other investments. The foundation is using low risk investments which tend to have low returns but are stable in performance and provide you with income month after month. If you look at this from the Network Marketing point of view it is where you will start building the structure of your business. Building each leg and achieving your promotions until you get to the stage where you have a stable business which will provide income every month.

Income – this is where you are adding investments with the purpose of producing regular monthly income. As the investment grows so does the income. When you have enough income you can move onto...

Growth – investing more money into growing the investment to the stage where it is almost self-supporting. With guaranteed income the growth area can include some riskier investments which could produce exponential growth and income.

Speculation – these are higher risk investments such as Forex, Spread trading, Options etc. that produce very high returns. These investments are very high risk. You can lose a lot of money in the blink of an eye. On the other hand, one investment that works often produces more money than you lose in all the other investments. Due to the high level of risk we only look at these types of investments once you have mastered the other three levels and have a solid base and plenty of Cashflow.

Mastering the Investment Pyramid

It takes time and patience to build and master the investment pyramid. Time learning the different types of investments, their little quirks and time learning the skills to be able to manage the investment.

It takes patience. Taking little steps every day in each category to learn and build. It takes patience to let the investment grow and start providing you with the security, income and growth you desire.

Patience to keep learning. I've been an investor for over 30 years. I am still learning. I still regularly go on training courses from my peers to see what is new in the markets. Markets change, legislation changes, demand changes, technology changes, people change. With each change there is more to learn. New techniques and skills to acquire. More fundamental and technical analysis to see if the investment is still doing what it was meant to do.

Be open to learning and continuous development and you will master the Investment Pyramid. Just remember what it was like starting to build your Network Marketing Business. It took lots of practice, patience and perseverance to master your business and start getting the results.

The Skills

There are 4 main skills to use in investing. These skills ensure you get the best possible benefits in the shortest timeframe.

Leverage – this is the number 1 skill to master. Learning to leverage generates wealth very quickly and will determine how quickly you reach financial independence and how quickly you become wealthy. The more you leverage the more income you can generate. Leverage can be used in all walks of life. You've probably used it to build your network marketing business by moving team members into different locations to get the best possible structure for your business. Have you ever found yourself about to sign a new team member and saying to them if you sign up I will put this person underneath you so you can start building your team straight away? That's using leverage. In the investment world we use leverage slightly differently but it's still used to get the best possible result.

Compounding Interest or Compounding Effect – Einstein said Compound Interest was the 8th wonder of the world. In shares you can use an aggressive form of compounding by generating income every month. Taking daily steps to make your investments work for you and produce regular income generates a compounding effect which produces results sooner rather than later. Having the patience to let the compounding effect kick in where patience, persistence and perseverance come in.

Income Producing Assets – most people spend a lifetime thinking they are buying assets when they are in fact, buying liabilities. I like the definition by Robert Kiyosaki, multimillionaire and author of Rich Dad, Poor Dad books about assets and liabilities as it is easy to remember. He says "an asset is something that puts money in your pocket. A liability is something that takes money out of your pocket." Learning the difference between investment assets and investment liabilities and you will always have money available if you practice buying or creating income producing assets.

Good Debt – the definition of Good Debt is any source of money you use to purchase income producing assets. If you buy something which doesn't generate income and you are using debt to buy it then it is bad debt. Debt such as Mortgages, Overdrafts, and Credit Cards used to buy income producing assets are good debt.

Balanced Investing

We've already covered that there are 4 Investment Categories – Property, Paper, Business and Cash. Investing in all 4 categories provides balanced investing which gives strength and protection to the investor during turbulent times.

I have seen many people who invested in just one category go bankrupt during recessions and especially the Great Recession of 2008. The reason they went bankrupt was because too much money was tied up in one category and they were unable to move their money from a downward investment to an upward investment.

In 2008, Property Investors were hit particularly hard. Some investors needed to sell their property to release cash or had pressure put on them buy mortgage companies to get rid of the properties due to negative equity as the house prices dropped. The investors had properties which were either selling low as house prices dropped or the investors did not have enough equity in the property to accept lower values so potential buyers could not get mortgages. The properties didn't sell. Many property investors found themselves getting deeper into debt because rents had dropped and they were short of money to cover mortgage repayments. Some investors were in such a bad situation they had no option but to file for bankruptcy.

During the Great Recession when property and shares were in a downward spiral, many people were made redundant, network marketing became a growth industry. It boomed.

Low start-up costs helped many of the unemployed move into self-employment and start earning again.

Investors who were in the four investment categories survived easier than those in just one. It was still tough but they had more strings to their bow and were able to shift money to where it was the most effective in generating more cash to support the other investments. For example, while property and shares were declining in value business such as network marketing were booming along with Gold and Silver Bullion. Investors who quickly moved money into Bullion made enormous returns. Prior to the Great Recession, Gold was trading around $400 a troy ounce during the recession it went up to just under $2000 a troy ounce. Those investors who were able to move money quickly into gold bullion made a lot of money in a short period of time.

In the picture below you can see how money can move between each category in whatever direction you want. This allows you to build in all 4 categories taking advantage of growth areas.

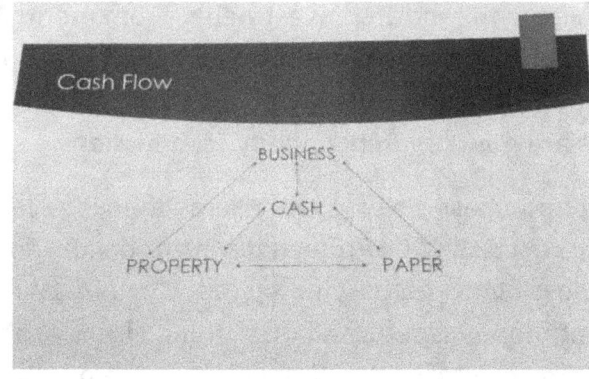

Having the ability to move money around will help you build wealth quicker. Remember moving cash around between each category will help you to build your wealth faster. Don't fall into the temptation of saying that's the share money it has to stay there. If there is a property or business deal and you need cash to do it sell the shares. Make sure you have cash for the next deal.

Fast Cash

I have an expression which I call Fast Cash. What I mean from this is how quickly you can put money into an investment and get it back out.

When I started my Utility Warehouse network marketing business it cost me £199 to join. In those bad old days (lol 2011) I had to sign up six customers before I earned any commission. It took me just 2 months to earn enough cash to repay the £199 I had spent to join UW. That money was then available for another investment. From month 3 I was making profit. That is infinite profit as I no longer had any money tied up in the business. All costs relating to the business are now covered with my commissions.

I recently purchased a Spanish Villa as a holiday let. That purchase cost £13,000. Projected returns on lets are that it will be possible to get my money back within 12 months. Once that money is returned everything else is profit and I will have my capital back to reinvest into the next project.

I'm an Angel Investor. By this I mean I help new businesses start up and in exchange I receive shares in the business. Sometimes I give cash and sometimes I help put systems in place within the business.

When I've given cash to a business there is always an exit strategy. That strategy is that I must receive my investment plus interest back within 3-5 years. I keep the money flowing.

Whatever business or property investment you are doing you want to know how quickly you will get your money back. The quicker the return, the quicker you can put it into the next investment. This is Fast Cash.

Mind-set

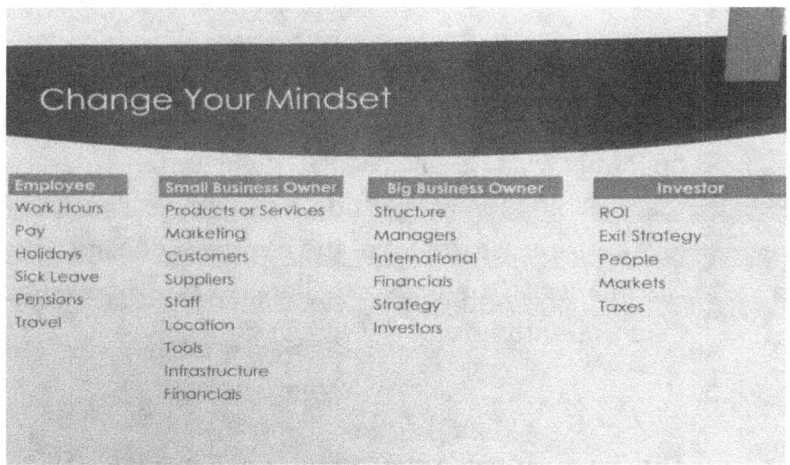

The picture above shows 4 different mind-sets. As a Network Marketer you start as a small business owner working through the Big Business Owner category until you become an investor.

The different mind-sets are:

1. **The Employee** - as an employee while they work for the company and are dedicated to the company, the focus is about the employee. How much will I be paid? What holidays will I be entitled to? Sick leave, pensions, travel time, work hours are just some of the questions the employee will ask about the benefits that working for the company will provide for themselves before accepting a job. Once employed they will be thinking about overtime and pay rises.

2. **The Small Business Owner** – is a jack of all trades. They need to know about products and services and how they will be delivered to the customer. They are responsible for marketing, staff, the business location, infrastructure of the business, dealing with the financials, there are a million and one things that take their attention.

3. **The Big Business Owner** – has managers and staff to run the business so they only need to focus on the structure of the business, whether it will be local or international, financials, taxes and who they want as investors in their business. In the case of Network Marketers you have a team below you all focusing

on building their own businesses which in the process will build your business. You also have the company you work for who provide the structure, products and services.

The fourth mind-set is **The Investor**. Your focus as an investor will be

1. **ROI** – what the return on investment (ROI) is going to be.

    I recently put together a Peer-to-Peer deal. A group of people within the Mastermind Groups contributed to the deal. The money was loaned to an existing business which was moving to new premises. I negotiated the deal over 2 years at 6% per annum interest rate with capital and interest repaid each month. It was interesting to see the mind-set reaction from members. One said 6% was too low they wanted a higher return. In effect, they were earning 12% as it was 6% per annum. Another didn't want their money tied up for 2 years. Capital was being repaid on a pro-rata basis monthly. Whereas in reality within 12 months half their capital would have been returned. If you include interest more than half their original investment would have been returned. Although the loan is based over 24 months the full capital is repaid in 21 months and the final 3 months of repayments are interest.

So a word of caution - When you look at the ROI make sure you analyse all the facts you have in front of you carefully ensuring you have all the correct information on which to base your decision.

2. **Exit Strategy** – how quickly will I get my money back so I can move it into the next opportunity? This is a very important consideration.

I have already mentioned how quickly I was able to get my investment back from the Networking Business. It took 2 months. Today everything I earn from my Networking Business is infinite return. It may only be small as I don't work the business to the extent it needs to be. The business owes me nothing as I've had back everything I put in to get started. Today it is all free money I receive each month.

My property portfolio is the same. I borrowed £300 on a credit card and used that to pay the legal fees on a property deal. I negotiated a 100% financed deal for the property. The property was refurbished and the money released from the growth value. That money was used to repay the £300 and provide a deposit on the next property. Today I have a £10 million property portfolio and I do not have any of my own money in the portfolio. Every month I collect tens of thousands of pounds in rental income which is free money. The value of the portfolio is growing. Again this is free money.

In the share portfolio I have some shares which are invested in for growth. When the shares double in value, I sell half the shares and recoup the initial investment. Then any profit on the remaining shares is infinite because I have none of my money left in the shares.

The exit strategy ensures I have no personal money left in the investment. I have Fast Cash which means I can invest quicker into other investment opportunities as they arise.

3. **People** – who are the people I want to partner with or have joint ventures with.

   There is a saying in the newer version of the movie The Italian Job. "It's not the person I don't trust it's the devil inside them." It's a great quote. Who are the people you most want to do business with? The ones who are like minded and trustworthy who you have built a relationship with. Or the guy from the pub who has the next hot tip for the 2pm race at Ascot or is selling an item that fell off the back of a truck. You know the type of people I mean. Partnering with people is very much a trust relationship. Know who you are partnering with. Today, I do deals with people within my mastermind groups. People who have proven themselves capable of building investments, creating wealth and getting stuck in and taking action every day and building successful investments.

4. **Markets** – what are the markets doing? Where are we in the Investment Cycle? Building your own data and monitoring where you think you are in the investment cycle can give you the edge over other investors so you are ahead of the investment opportunities instead of following the sheep. Have confidence in your own ability to read the markets. The so called "experts" are wrong more times than they are right. Ignore what they say. You will have as much skill as them if not more, by the end of this book, to be able to judge where an investment is today in the Investment Cycle.

5. **Taxes** – how can I legally reduce tax liabilities? We all hate them, loathe them but there is no escaping the fact we have to pay them. The question is how can you legally pay less in taxes? The Stocks and Shares ISA is one way which is perfectly legal to do. The government allows you to invest up to x amount each year into an ISA. For 2017/18 tax year that is £20,000. How much money do you think you can earn per year tax free if you are putting £20,000 a year into an ISA. A 10% return would give you £2000 and that is easily achievable. At 10% you have just earned £2000 tax free. You can then invest that back into your ISA. This allows you to invest more than £20,000 into the ISA. The compounding effect means that within a few years you could be earning

more in tax free income per year than your ISA allowance. Tax free income which is encouraged by the government and perfectly legal. However, through the £2.73 Club we teach you how to earn 30%+ per annum from your shares. For a £20,000 investment that return becomes £6,000 plus the following year that is more as you allow the compounding effect to kick in. There are several ISA investors who have managed to generate over £1 million in there ISA tax free just by using simple strategies.

As an Angel Investor, I invest into businesses which qualify under government schemes. These are schemes such as SEIS and EIS. These schemes mean that I get a deduction off my tax bill equivalent to 50% or 25% of the money I have paid into the new business. If I put £1000 into an SEIS approved new business I get £500 off my tax bill. The government is encouraging me to invest in new start-up businesses in return for reducing my tax bill. Also, with SEIS I get zero capital gains tax on any profit I make through the growth of the business provided I meet the government's criteria when I sell my shares. As an Angel Investor the government is providing me with zero rate tax incentives or reduced tax incentives to take a risk which can make enormous profit for me if the company is successful.

Understanding the incentives from government to reduce tax liabilities is part of the mind-set of an investor.

Your mind-set will change and you will think differently as you start investing. Be prepared for the change. You won't notice it yourself but others will. Peter is my business partner but before that he was a client of the £2.73 club. His mind-set changed when he started learning about investing. So great was the change that several of his friends became clients. I kept hearing "I want some of what Pete is doing". Pete's mind-set and his outlook had totally changed.

As you start the change in mind-set you will start to see the opportunities around you and wonder how you missed them in the first place. You are starting to become an Investor.

Investment Cycles

Every investment has a natural cycle when the investment is popular and not so popular. When prices are high and prices are low. You need to be looking at investments that are in the low part of the cycle and ready to take off in value.

In the chart below you can see the natural cycle of an investment.

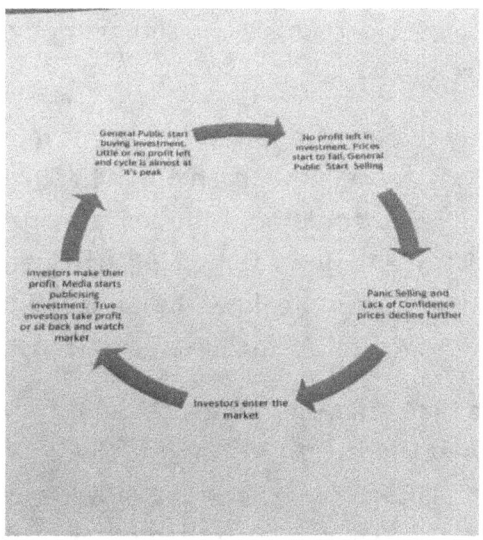

The question I am always asked is how do you know the cycle is at the bottom and ready to go up? It would be lovely to say I have a crystal ball that says invest now. It doesn't work that way. What I do is look at what the markets are doing and assess where I think that investment is in the cycle. Then cross my fingers, take a deep breath and hope like hell the investment has reached the turning point.

When analysing an investment I always assume that it might go down slightly when I buy it. Be prepared. If it does go down don't panic. It will go back up. Your timing just wasn't quite perfect but you'll get it right next time.

Investment cycles vary in time for each investment. The gold bullion cycle can last decades. Property investments usually work over a recession whether that be a year, 5 years or a decade.

Once you buy the investment at the low level sit back and wait for it to grow and either cash out at the high or as close as you can. Or you could hold the investment and let the next cycle kick in and do its thing. It is unusual for a low to go down below a previous low. Inflation, usually ensures the low is higher than the last time.

For example. I purchased property in 2002 for £35,000 the property went up to £120,000 by 2007. During the recession the value dropped and the new low was £95,000. More than £60,000 higher than the previous low. Property prices are again rising. Who knows where the new high will be. Already house prices are higher than the 2007 price. There's probably room for them to go even higher. I wouldn't be surprised if the new high isn't around £150,000+ for that particular property. Just watch the cycles and see what happens. Be realistic don't expect the property to drop back down to £35,000 as that is highly unlikely to happen. Buy when you have the best opportunity and the best deal.

Summary

This section covers the basics of investing. That is the skills that need to be mastered to build a successful investment portfolio. As a Network Marketer you will have noticed that you already possess some of the skills. You learnt those through building your business. You learnt them through trial and error. Finding out what worked for you and what didn't as you built your business. The same applies to investing. Finding what works and what doesn't. Using a mentor to show you the best way forward. The £2.73 Club can be that mentor.   With a range of training and investment programs to suit most people who want to learn to invest.

4 Category Investing

Property Investing

Find your Niche

There are many different types of property investing. For example if you wanted to invest in Residential property you could invest in apartments, flats, houses, student lets, houses of multiple occupation (HMO). Within each of those categories are subcategories.

If we took houses there are terraced houses; semi-detached; detached ranging from one bedroom upwards.

The skill for investing is to find a niche (a specific type of property) that suits you and stick to it.

Each property category has its own rules and regulations and it is easier to understand one particular category rather than trying to master them all.

Think of your Network Marketing Business. You can name almost any product and find a Network Marketing Business for it. Within the £2.73 Club we have many Network Marketers who have businesses in Utilities, Cosmetics, Skincare, Essential Oils, Household gadgets, Food, Household Cleaners, Gold the list goes on and on. So, why do you stick with the Company you chose? The answer is simple. You found a niche that you like. One that fitted you and you decided would be the best company for you to work with. Property is the same. Find the niche that suits you and stick with it.

One of our members in the £2.73 Club likes single garages. She buys, renovates and then rents out the garages. That is her niche in property investing. It's low cost to buy the garages. There is no mortgage. Renovation costs are low and she finds it easy to get long term renters.

My daughter's niche is "rent-to-buy" on overseas properties. She buys properties that are difficult for the owner to sell and buys them using a rent-to-buy scheme. Under the rent-to-buy the current owner in effect becomes the mortgagee. She pays them an agreed amount each month that is deducted from the cost of the property. Over an agreed period of time the property is paid for. She then rents out the properties, some as holiday lets and others on long term lets. Once the rent-to-buy period is over (usually 10 years) she owns a mortgage free property which has been paid for through rents. This is low cost to start.

Normally, she has a finder's fee (that is she pays people to find the property and put the deal in place for her) and the solicitor's fee.

My niche is UK family homes 2-5 bedroom houses. Families tend to stay in one place longer as their kids are going through school. Working families provide the stability I want and are less hassle. I have bought a lot of properties by using a deposit and buy-to-let mortgage. The mortgage is for 25 years and depending on the type of mortgage either totally paid off at the end of the 25 years (capital and interest) or has to be repaid at the end of the term (Interest only)

How to Invest In Property

Cash – you can pay cash for an investment. If you opt for a smaller property investment such as garages, storage units etc. then cash is the best way to invest.

Mortgage – for larger purchases while you might have the cash available, remember the first skill for wealth, Leverage. If you have a large sum of money to invest in property use a buy-to-let mortgage and split your money to buy several properties. In today's market £100,000 could with the help of a mortgage buy you 3-4 properties. This generates more income and helps you invest in more properties as a quicker rate. This builds your wealth faster.

Lease Option – a lease option gives you the right to buy a property within a given timeframe for a set price. For example you may want to buy a house that is worth

£80,000. The owner is in no rush to sell and happy for you to rent the property. The owner gives you the option to buy the property during the next 10 years for an agreed amount of £100,000. You then have 10 years in which to decide to purchase that property. In the meantime, you use the property as though you own it. You can rent it, you insure it and you maintain it. In exchange the owner receives an agreed payment from you each month. Usually the payment covers any mortgage on the property plus provides the owner with a little something for themselves. You rent the property as though you own it and receive the rent less the payment to the owner. This is a great way to get into property investing without actually owning a property.

Rent-to-Rent – this type of property investment works well with larger properties such as HMO. (House of multiple occupation). With rent-to-rent the owner of the property gives you the right to rent out the property. In effect you become the letting agent. However, instead of receiving commissions as a letting agent would you receive the rent in full? If there is a mortgage you cover the cost of the mortgage plus something for the owner. You are responsible for insurance, compliances and maintenance.

Rent-to-buy – is where you agree to buy a property. The owner provides the mortgage on the property. You pay rent to the owner each month and either part or all the rental payment is deducted from the price of the property. At the end of the agreed term you either own the property outright or you have to raise a smaller mortgage to purchase the property. There is a lot of scope to be able to negotiate a deal which suits both you and the seller.

Delayed Completion – is where you exchange contracts to buy a property paying the vendor a deposit. You then extend the completion date for a set period of time. The period is agreed between you and the vendor but can be up to several years. You are the owner of the property from exchange of contract so have the use of the property. You are also required to maintain it and insure it. The final price on the property less the deposit is paid on the agreed completion date.

Joint Venture – is where you partner with other people to complete a deal on a property. Your partners and you contribute to the purchase of the property. The contribution can be finance, skills and/or knowledge.

Summary

Using a combination of some the strategies above will help you get the best out of your capital and keep Cashflow moving.

I have some properties on buy-to-let mortgages, property on lease option and property on rent to buy. Using this combination of strategies gives me use of and control of more properties than I would normally have been able to purchase without tying up capital. It also allows me to generate more Cashflow without having to use capital to do it.

Paper Investing

Paper Investing is anything for which you hand over your money and receive a receipt in return. However, rather than just handing our money over to other people to invest we prefer to have some control over what happens with our money for that reason the preference is Shares and Bonds.

Bonds

There are two main types of bonds we use for investing. Treasury Bonds and Corporate Bonds. As a starter Treasury Bonds are the easiest to invest in and the safest. In the UK you can invest in Treasury Bonds through NS&I website. (Note: these are not premium bonds which are gambling not investing). Treasury Bonds are guaranteed by the Government and you can invest up to £1 million. There are a variety of Bonds that offer monthly income or capital growth.

It's worth remembering with Treasury Bonds they pay very low return. They are secure and for that reason form part of the foundation of investing on our Investment Pyramid.

Corporate Bonds are riskier and you can lose some or all of your money. They are traded through most stock market platforms. Crowdfunding platforms such as Crowdcube have their own customers who offer corporate bonds. Interest rates vary from low to high. The higher the rate usually means the riskier the Bond.

Councils are another source of investment bonds. Councils will offer bonds for a fixed period while they are raising funds for specific projects. These are again low return but fairly safe.

Shares

Date	Share Price	Share Bought	Total Shares	Average Cost per Share
January	50p	200	200	50p
February	53p	188	388	51.5p
March	45p	222	610	0.49p
April	47p	212	822	0.48p
May dividend reinvested into shares £10	45p	22	844	0.47p
May	45p	222	1066	0.46p
June	45p	222	1288	0.46p
July	47p	212	1500	0.46p
August	45p	222	1722	0.46p
September	50p	200	1922	0.45p
October Dividend reinvested into shares £25	50p	50	1972	0.45p
October	47p	212	2184	0.45p
November	40p	250	2434	0.45p
December	42p	238	2672	0.44p

I have to confess share investing is a favourite of mine. You can start with small sums of money and build a portfolio very quickly. Through the £2.73 Club we tend to use a Stocks and Shares ISA to invest as this negates income tax which would normally be paid on share dividends.

The most common strategies we use are: PCA, VCA and Buy Sell Zones.

PCA – Price Cost Averaging is the strategy of investing a set amount of money every month into one or two shares.

Example

In the example below £100 is used to buy shares in XYZ Company every month over a year. Dividends are only paid twice a year.

Share prices have fluctuated during the year from a high of 53p to a low of 40p. By staggering the purchases over a year and reinvesting the dividend the share owes the investor 44p. Shares can be sold for 44p or a higher price for a profit.

This strategy is low risk and will generally produce a capital gain of around 5%.

VCA – is Variable Cost Averaging. This strategy is still buying into shares every month but if the shares are up in value use on 75% of your investment money. If the shares are down in value use your total pot of investment money.

Example –

VCA
Value Cost Averaging
Month 1

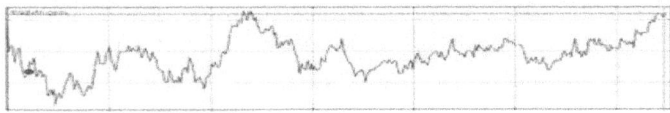

In the above chart you can see the price of the share goes up and down. When the share is high instead of using your full £100 to invest you would instead buy £75 worth of shares. The following month if the price of the shares is down buy £125 worth of shares (that is the £25 held over from the previous month plus your normal £100)

This strategy will on average produce a 15% capital growth.

Buy Sell Zones – this strategy requires a little bit more work in investing and monitoring but can produce higher percentage returns.

Buy & Sell Zones

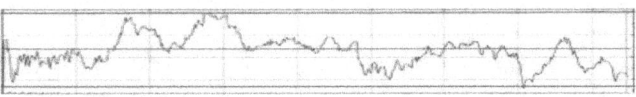

For buy sell zones we use charts. Draw a line at the highest price level and another at the lowest price level then a 3rd line through the centre. When share prices are in the bottom half buy shares. When they are in the top half sell shares. This strategy will produce around 25% return average per annum.

Summary

While there are many types of investments that fall within the Paper Category Bonds and Shares are the preferred options as we have more control over the investment. Bonds provide stable low interest returns. Treasury Bonds are guaranteed by Government up to £1 Million. Shares can produce much higher yields but will take some extra monitoring. The three strategies PCA, VCA and Buy Sell Zones are the easiest and least time consuming investments.

Cash

Gold & Silver Bullion

One of the best cash investments are Gold and Silver Bullion.

History

Throughout history people have traded or bartered for goods. If you have some apples to sell and I have some wine you want to purchase bartering would determine how many apples were equivalent to a bottle of wine.

The Romans introduced silver coins as a currency in lieu of bartering. They determined that the apples were worth so much silver and a piece of silver would be clipped off the coin to pay for the apples.

In later years a piece of paper promising to pay the bearer a sum of money became the norm for paying for goods. The paper was backed up with Gold and Silver in storage so the owner did not have to carry large sacks of coins around with them.

Up until the late 1970's all reserve banks held Gold and Silver in their basements equivalent to the amount of currency that was in circulation. So, when you accepted a pound note you knew you could go to the Bank of England and ask for one pound in gold or silver. No one ever did.

In the late 1970's Richard Nixon, as president of the United States, made it law that the United States no longer needed bullion reserves to back up paper notes. It wasn't long until other countries did the same.

Today, while some Reserve Banks still hold some bullion reserves most countries just issue paper with a promise to pay the bearer. There is no longer any security value in a note. There is only the assumption that the note is worth what it says it is and will buy you to buy goods to the value of the note.

Bullion Today

Today Bullion is a separate investment opportunity. An investment that has become a safe haven in times of trouble.

Bullion is a commodity similar to copper and platinum traded on an exchange and revalued with every trade. US dollars is the bench mark for buying bullion.

When I first started buying bullion Gold traded at $400 a troy ounce and Silver at $8 a troy ounce. (Troy ounce is the weight of a coin. In normal standards 1 ounce equals 28.3 grams. In bullion investing a troy ounce is 31.03 grams). Today, as I write this, Gold is trading at $1281.30 a troy ounce and silver is $18.040 a troy ounce.

The increase in value is due to several factors.

1. **Inflation** – natural inflation has meant the value of Gold and Silver has gone up to ensure the intended value remains intact. By that I mean the ability to buy goods remains the same. For example if one ounce of silver bought you a barrel of apples 20 years ago. Today you would not be very happy is one ounce of silver only bought you 1 apple. Gold and silver are automatically revalued to inflation.
2. **Economic Difficulties** – In uncertain times when investors become worried about the value of paper currency they move money into bullion as a safe haven. In recent years that safe haven has become more used as we have had to deal with the Credit Crunch and Great Depression of 2008.

Today Britain again faces very uncertain economic times. There is tremendous volatility in the value of property, shares and other types of investments.

We have seen the highest unemployment on record in 2009 become the lowest level of unemployment since the 1970's. Yet people are still struggling to pay for basic needs – a roof over their head and food on the table. Paper currency does not have the value it had several years ago. You only have to watch the economic news to see that today's wages are not buying as much as they did a year ago. So, Investors look for the best place to protect the value of their money and for that reason they are continuing to buy gold and silver to protect themselves.

In June 2016 there was the vote to leave the EU, known as Brexit. There were doom and gloom forecasts of the impact the Brexit Vote would have on the economy. The day after the referendum panic started and shares prices fell then recovered. Exchange rates dropped and then recovered.

In the midst of all this panic the price of Gold and Silver bullion went up. Every time there is something negative in the economic market or which is expected to affect global economies the price of Gold and Silver goes up.

The threat of war with North Korea sees the price of Gold and Silver go up every time a rocket is launched.

For centuries Gold and Silver Bullion have been a safe haven in times of economic turbulence. Today, is no different, it is still a safe haven.

Gold or Silver Bullion

As with all investments it is a personal choice of whether you hold Gold or Silver Bullion or both. Both move up and down in value depending on what is happening in the markets.

Gold can be purchased in bars and coins. Bars start small at 1 gram. Buying today you can get a gold 1 gram bar for around £45. As a starter investing in 1 gram Gold Bars gives you the opportunity to buy small amounts of bullion at an affordable price.

Silver is also available in bars and coins. I troy ounce bullion coin is available for around £20 again allowing you to purchase on a regular basis for a small amount.

Bars or coins in either Gold or Silver comes down to your preference just ensure they are from a genuine dealer and stamped as 999.9% pure.

Where to buy your Bullion

You can buy from any supplier you choose as long as you ensure that you are buying genuine investment bars and coins.

Don't get trapped into thinking this is coin collecting. It isn't. Coin collecting also known as numismatic collections is the collection of coins with a trading value determined between two parties. For example there are special minted 50p coins that are rare and have a value higher than face value. These are special coins for coin investors. The coins have no investment value from our point of view as they are most likely nickel or combined metals that were once in circulation as a currency.

Bullion is a treasury issued bar or coin that is 999.9% pure. It is recognised investment grade and is traded on its own platform based on the current price for gold and silver bullion. Most countries issue their own bullion. In the UK you have Britannia; America has the American Eagle, Canada has the Maple Leaf etc. There are also bullion investment coins such as Star Wars Collections and the Marvel Collections.   These coins are bullion grade investment coins where a limited number of coins are in circulation. These coins are expected over time to be worth more than the bullion value due to limited numbers.

Storage

As you start buying bullion it will be in small quantities. Therefore, storage at home is the best starting point. If you have a home safe that would be best.   If not find somewhere safe and secure for storage.

If you start buying large quantities then it may be safer to use bullion storage facilities.

Peer – to – Peer Lending

What is P2P?

Simply it is a group of people coming together to lend a sum of money to another person. In return they receive interest and/or capital back each month until the debt is paid off in full. In effect, you become the bank for the borrower.

How Does It Work?

Each investor contributes money to a pot. It can be as little as £10 to as much as you want. In some cases private P2P some investors will put in a million or two depending on the project. The pot is then given to a borrower under certain terms and conditions with any security needed. The borrower then uses the money for the purpose intended.

Each month or as designated the lenders receive interest payments. Sometimes payments can be interest only or interest and capital. The loan is for a pre-determined period at which time the loan should be repaid in full or refunded.

Business

Lifestyle

I have left business as the last investment category because you are already a successful business owner by building your Network Marketing business. I have no intention of trying to teach you about business.

As a Network Marketer you are building a business which offers enormous opportunities, wealth and rewards. It is a business which can help you achieve your dream lifestyle. For me, that is the most important part of being an investor – I am able to have the lifestyle of my dreams.

While I am a network marketer, the company I work with is UK based so I have chosen to keep it as a small part of my overall business/investment portfolio preferring to focus on the type of businesses/investments I can run from anywhere in the world.

As part of my lifestyle, I have chosen to have a couple of overseas homes. My business model allows me to work for just one week a month and spend the remainder of the month at a location to suit me – my home in UK; at my apartment skiing the in French Alps or at my villa basking in the Spanish Sun. My investments ensure I have sufficient time and money to relax and enjoy the lifestyle I have chosen.

My Businesses/Investment Model

Speaker – my speaking business is based around how often I feel like speaking. Seminars are a mainstay of my business model. Holding my own seminars I get to choose how often I speak and where. I run investment workshops and these are held in the first week of the month. Webinars are also first week of the month ensuring I am free for the remainder of the month.

Author – as an author I have written 15 books in as many years. All are 'how to' books which are sold worldwide. America, Canada, New Zealand, Australia and Japan are my most successful markets. I'm able to write anywhere with my laptop and an internet connection. I write modules for long term training courses and online courses. I also produce 'how to' content for people who want their own books and products but are unable to produce it themselves.

Property – As a property investor I have a large managed portfolio. By managed I mean I have a letting agent who manages my properties for me. This provides regular monthly income which comes in every month no matter where I am in the world. It also means the agent is paid to ensure my properties are looked after. If you've read any of my other books you will know I am averse to letting agents because they have always let me down in the past. It has taken 17 years but I finally found one I could trust to manage the properties for me.

Shares – I have an ISA Stocks and Shares account which is used as a pension. It provides a monthly income and covers my annual tax bill.

Angel Investor – As an Angel Investor I have used tax breaks to invest in start-up companies. I currently invest in several companies which provide dividends and capital growth on my investments.

RKN Publishing – this business was set up to publish my own books. It is used to help first time authors get their book to the market. I receive a commission based on their sales.

£2.73 Club - the £2.73 Club is a business set up to teach investment skills. Through this we have helped many people start their own Network Marketing Business; Other Businesses in the UK; a Property portfolio in both the UK and Overseas; Share Market Investment Accounts; Bullion investment and P-2-P investments. We help people, like you, go from Zero to Millionaire.

CC Events – is an Event Management business which runs my own events plus events for other organisations. I'm a partner in this business with my daughter and Peter Rowlands.

Tiroka – is a brand name used as an umbrella for several businesses including a Lease Option business, property maintenance, health and beauty and general retail.

This overall business model may seem a lot of work but actually, allows me a great deal of freedom to work as I want to and when I want to. It starts with having a great base from which to work. For you that base is Network Marketing which provides the income to be able to reinvest into other areas which in turn allows you to build multiple streams of income with very little effort.

Passive Income

As a Network Marketer your focus is on building a business which provides passive/residual income. Investments are another way to continue building passive income without reducing the time you put into building your business. Yes, you need a little time to maintain the investment but on the whole you will need around an hour a month to for each investment. Once set up it adds to your overall income and provides another layer of wealth and lifestyle. It's a buffer against difficult economic times.

Summary

Build businesses and investments that require little time and effort but provide multiple streams of income. Build your business around the lifestyle you want. Outsource where necessary.

Getting Started

Investment Pyramid

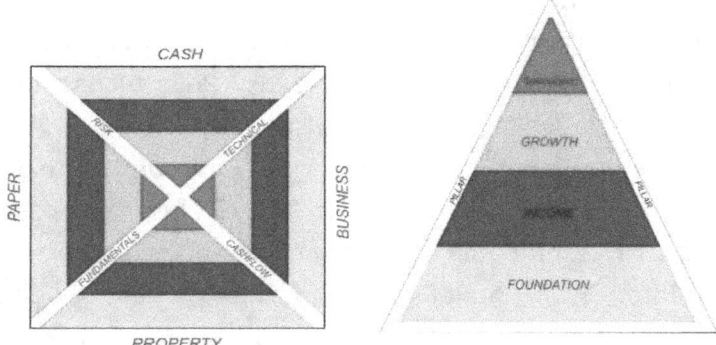

At the start of this book, I wrote about building an Investment Pyramid. The four sides of the Pyramid being Business, Property, Paper and Cash. I introduced you to the 4 support pillars and the 4 layers of the Pyramid. I hope it has whet your appetite to learn more about investing.

As a Network Marketer you are successfully building the business side of your pyramid. Now to ensure stability in volatile and difficult economic times you need to build the other sides of your pyramid.

The greatest investors of our time – Warren Buffett; Richard Branson; Bill Gates; Jeff Bezos and Michael Bloomberg have all built successful businesses and invested in the 4 categories of the pyramid. You have the chance to join them. You are already on the way with your Network Marketing business.

The £2.73 Club

The £2.73 Club offers training to ensure you build a balanced investment portfolio. We run seminars, workshops and webinars to help you start building your wealth and lifestyle. We have an array of modular training and online training to suit your needs. Private coaching is also available visit us at www.facebook.com/273clublimited to find out more. You can also join our Facebook group "£2.73 Club" for tips and blogs on investing. Join a growing number of members who are intent on building their lifestyle and wealth. https://www.facebook.com/groups/1032901670065445/?ref=group_browse_new

Seminars:-

From Zero to Millionaire – a one day introduction to investing. This event is free to attend. VIP tickets are available at a small charge. The VIP ticket includes lunch and a "goodie" bag. We have several speakers who are all successful in their field. We cover all four categories of investing and how you can get started.

The Next Step – is a 2/3 day seminar going into greater detail than the 1 day seminar. It provides training in all 4 categories of the investment pyramid. There is a charge for this event and attendees would benefit from attending the From Zero to Millionaire event although it is not necessary.

Details of our seminars and dates can be found on www.facebook.com/273clublimited

Online Training Modules:-

Our original training program has written modules and is supported with videos providing a step-by-step route to building your wealth and lifestyle. A one off membership fee entitles you to all the content which you can work through at your own pace. Contact us via www.facebook.com/273clublimited

Private Coaching

Our private coaching program provides one on one support to get you to millionaire faster and help you build your dream lifestyle quicker. You have access to joint ventures and one-off deals only available to our private clients. Contact us via www.facebook.com/273clublimited for more information

Millionaire Plus Club

Our Millionaire Plus Club is for serious investors who have proven they know how to invest and become millionaires. This club offers access to higher level joint ventures and investment opportunities. It is the next step up for investors who have been through our other programs.

Summary

As a network marketer you have the skills to build a successful business and one side of the investment pyramid. But to survive in uncertain economic conditions you also need to have a balanced investment strategy. 4 Category investing provides the balance to achieve this.

Enjoy your journey to greater wealth and don't forget to build your dream lifestyle along the way.

Thank you for reading this book and if we can help you on your journey visit us at

www.facebook.com/273clublimited

www.ingramcontent.com/pod-product-compliance
Lightning Source LLC
Chambersburg PA
CBHW030050230526
45471CB00003B/1032